SEE MY LOVELY
POISON IVY

SEE MY LOVELY POISON IVY

POISON IVY

And Other Verses About Witches, Ghosts and Things by Lilian Moore

Pictures by Diane Dawson

ATHENEUM   1975   NEW YORK

To Jean Karl

3 6001 00001 3975

LIBRARY OF CONGRESS CATALOGING IN PUBLICATION DATA
Moore, Lilian.   See my lovely poison ivy.
SUMMARY: Short poems about ghosts, bats,
monsters, witches, and Halloween.
1. Halloween—Juvenile poetry. [1. Halloween—Poetry]
I. Dawson, Diane. II. Title.   PZ8.3.M7835Se   811'.5'4   75-8581
ISBN 0-689-30468-4

The Ghost in Our Apartment House, Cat,
Something Is There, A Teeny Tiny Ghost, Johnny Drew a Monster
and *The Witch's Song* reprinted by permission of
Scholastic Magazines, Inc. from *Spooky Rhymes*
and Riddles, text © 1972 by Lilian Moore

Text copyright © 1975 by Lilian Moore
Pictures copyright © 1975 by Diane Dawson
All rights reserved
Published simultaneously in Canada by
McClelland & Stewart, Ltd.
Manufactured in the United States of America
Printed by The Murray Printing Company
Forge Village, Massachusetts
Bound by H. Wolff, New York
First Edition

CONTENTS

.

SEE MY LOVELY
POISON IVY

BEDTIME STORIES

"Tell me a story,"
Says Witch's Child.

"About the Beast
So fierce and wild.

About a Ghost
That shrieks and groans.

A Skeleton
That rattles bones.

About a Monster
Crawly-creepy.

Something nice
To make me sleepy."

SHADOWS

Is there a place where
shadows go
when it is
dark?

Do they play
in the
park?
Slip down slides?

Stride down streets?
Stretch high?
Shrink thin?

Do they spin
in the wind and
fly
with leaves?

Splash in the
rain?
Hang up to
dry?

Do they miss us?
Are they
glad
to see the sun—or
sad?

WHOOO?

WHO . . . OOO?
said the owl
in the dark old tree.

WHEEEEEEEEEEEE!
said the wind
with a howl.
WHEEEEEEEEEEEEE!

WHO . . . OOOOOO?
WHEEEEE . . . EEEE!

WHOOOOOO?
WHEEEEEEE!

They didn't
scare
each other,
but they did
scare
WHOOO?
Me!

SAID A LONG CROCODILE

Said a very l—o—n—g crocodile,
"My length is a terrible trial!
    I know I should diet
    But each time I try it
I'm hungry for more than a mile!"

LITTLE UGH

Witch's daughter,
Little Ugh,
Went out to
Trick or Treat.

At every door
She hollered
"I WANT SOMETHING
TO EAT!"

At every house
The people said,
"My, you are a fright!
What a scary costume!
It's the best one out
tonight!"

FOG

Oh this is
Witches' Weather—
swirling
misting—
Oh this is
Witches' Weather
so don't go out
today!

They'll
wrap you round
in cobwebs—
curling
twisting—
They'll
wrap you round
in cobwebs
and you'll
never
find your
way!

Halloo!
Halloo!

I'm here.

Where are *you*?

CAT

Cat,
Cat,
Your eyes are bright and green,
Where have you been
What have you done
So skittery-scary this Hallowe'en?

And where did you get
that pointed hat?
Tell me *that*,
Cat!

THE WITCH'S SONG

Hey! Cackle! Hey!
Let's have fun today.
    All shoelaces will have knots.
    No knots will untie.
    Every glass of milk will spill.
    Nothing wet will dry.
    Every pencil point will break.
    And everywhere in town
    Peanut-buttered bread will drop
    Upside down!
Hey! Hey! Hey!
Have a pleasant day!

WHALE FOOD

A Whale liked to eat portions double.
Nothing he ate gave him trouble.
    But he just couldn't cope
    With *two* bars of soap.
And he now blows a whale of a bubble.

LOST AND FOUND

LOST:
A Wizard's loving pet.
Rather longish.
Somewhat scaly.
May be hungry or
upset.
Please feed daily.

P.S. Reward.

FOUND:
A dragon
breathing fire.
Flails his scaly
tail
in ire.
Would eat twenty LARGE meals
daily
if we let him.
PLEASE
Come and get him.

P.S. No reward necessary.

THE TROLL BRIDGE

This is the Bridge
of the
Terrible Troll.
No one goes
by
without paying
a toll,
a terrible toll
to the Troll.

It's no place to
loll, to
linger or
stroll,
to sing or to
play.

So if ever you
ride
to the
opposite side,
be ready to
pay
the terrible troll—
I mean terrible toll—
to the Terrible Toll—
I mean Troll.

WHY?

Why does the clock
go ticking away
with the
teeniest
tickety-tick
all day?
And then at night
when there *isn't*
a light,
why does the clock
go
Tock-Tock-Tock
TOCKETY-TOCKETY
TOCK-TOCK
TOCK?

DEAR COUNTRY WITCH

Dear Country Witch,

Come try our
city Halloween.
It's
keener
meaner
Halloweener!

What if yours
is
greener?
We'll climb
through smoke and
dust and
grime
upon my
vacuum cleaner.

City Witch

I WISH

"I wish,"
Said Baby Bat,
"That I could get
A Boy or Girl
To have me
For a pet.

We'd live
Inside this cold
Old cave
Safe from sunny weather,
Swooping out in
Darkest night
To feed on bugs
Together.

Then
Hanging in our
Cave we'd stay
Playing upside down
All day!"

FOOTPRINTS

It was snowing
Last night,
And today
I can see who came
This way.

A dog ran lightly here,
And a cat.
A rabbit hopped by and—
What was THAT?

A twelve-toed foot
Two yards wide?
Another step here
In just one stride?

It was snowing
Last night.
Who came past?
I'll never be knowing
For I am going
The OTHER way,
Fast.

DO GHOULS?

Do ghouls
go out
on a rainy day?

When it
splishes and
sploshes,
do
ghouls
wear
ghoul-oshes?

ABOUT A MONSTER-OUS TOOTHACHE

"My fang aches!" cried Monster. "Oh dear!"
He fled to the dentist in fear.
　　　"I need novocaine.
　　　I can't stand the pain!"
He moaned as he held back a tear.

SOMETHING IS THERE

Something is there
　there on the stair
　　coming down
　　　coming down
　　　　stepping with care.
　　　　Coming down
　　　　coming down
　　　　slinkety-sly.

Something is coming and wants to get by.

LOOK AT THAT!

Look at that!
Ghosts lined up
at the laundromat,
all around the
block.

Each has
bleach
and some
detergent.

Each one seems to
think it
urgent

to take a spin
in a
washing machine

before the
clock
strikes
Halloween!

NO TV

Little Ghost
cries.
Little Ghost
begs.
Nary
a good
does it do.
"No TV tonight!"
says Papa Ghost.
"The horror show
is too
scary."

BELLOWED THE OGRE

Bellowed the Ogre
With One Fiery Eye,
    "Ho!
    The Mightiest
    Monster
    Am
    I!"

Roared Dinosaur Rex,
"I'm not easy to vex,
    But I'll swat
    That
    Braggart
    When he goes
    By!"

Whispered the Wizard,
"Upon my gizzard!
    I'll make
    Ogre a
    Bullfrog
    And
    Rex a
    Lizard!"

I LEFT MY HEAD

I left my head
somewhere
today.
Put it down for
just
a minute.
Under the
table?
On a chair?
Wish I were
able
to say
where.
Everything I need
is
in it!

EMPTY HOUSE SONG

The house on the hill
Has been empty so long
That now it keeps singing
An empty-house song:
        "I have cobwebs
        like thick hair.
        My hinges twinge
        and creak.
        Through every
        broken window
        wild winds shriek.
        In my musty
        hallways,
        Things prowl, Things
        roam.
        Isn't there a
        ghost
        somewhere
        who wants a
        home?"

WE THREE

We three
went out on Halloween,
A Pirate
An Ape
A Witch between.

We went from door to door.

By the light
of the moon
these shadows were seen
A Pirate
An Ape
A Witch between
and—

Say, how did we get to be FOUR?

TEETH

Today
they gave me
eyes and
nose
and then,
above my
chin,
they gave me
TEE-TH
for my
grin.

Now
it's dark.
They light
me.
My candle glows,
Hooray!
See my
nose,
my eyes,
my
TEETH...
Why are they running
away?

THE GHOST
IN OUR APARTMENT
HOUSE

The ghost
in our apartment house
makes *everybody*
late.

He gets into the
elevator,
closes the
gate,
presses all the
buttons
from one to
eight,

rides
up
and
down
and
up
and
down

while all the people
wait.

I'M SKELETON

I'm the local Skeleton
who walks this
street.
This is my beat.
Beware!
I'm not very hairy
but I scare
everyone I meet.

People quiver
when they see me.
They flee me!
They shiver
if they must walk
alone.

Oops, there's a dog.
I must run.
His tail has a wag.
He wants to play tag.
And how he would like a
BONE!

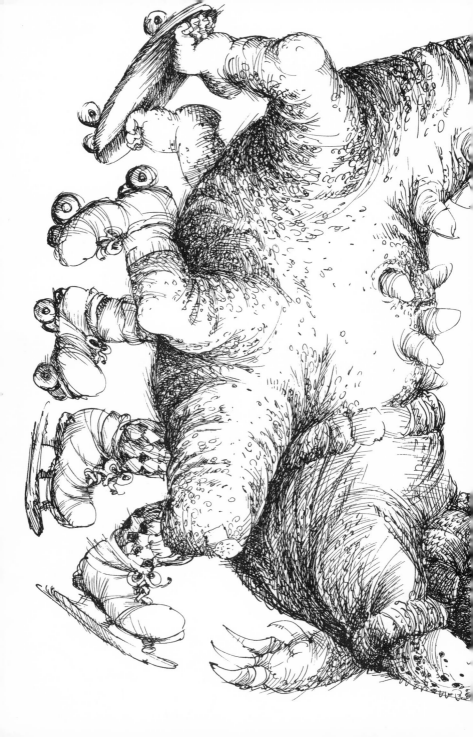

JOHNNY DREW A MONSTER

Johnny drew a monster.
The monster chased him.
Just in time
Johnny erased him.

NO ONE

In this room
there's not a
breeze.

No one sneezed
the littlest
sneeze.

No one wheezed
the faintest
wheeze.

The door's shut
tight
with a big brass
handle.

Who?
WHO
BLEW OUT THE CANDLE?

SAID THE MONSTER

Said the Monster, "You all think that I
Love to lunch on the folks who go by.
    If only you knew
    I'd much rather chew
On a peppery cheese pizza pie!"

WITCH GOES SHOPPING

Witch rides off
Upon her broom
Finds a space
To park it.
Takes a shiny shopping cart
Into the supermarket.
Smacks her lips and reads
The list of things she needs:

"Six bats' wings
Worms in brine
Ears of toads
Eight or nine.
Slugs and bugs
Snake skins dried
Buzzard innards
Pickled, fried."

Witch takes herself
From shelf to shelf
Cackling all the while.
Up and down and up and down and
In and out each aisle.
Out come cans and cartons
Tumbling to the floor.
"This," says Witch, now all a-twitch,
"Is a crazy store.
I CAN'T FIND A SINGLE THING
I AM LOOKING FOR!"

TEENY TINY GHOST

A teeny, tiny ghost
no bigger than a mouse,
at most,
lived in a great big house.

It's hard to haunt
a great big house
when you're a teeny tiny ghost
no bigger than a mouse,
at most.

He did what he could do.

So every dark and stormy night—
the kind that shakes a house with fright—
if you stood still and listened right,
you'd hear a
teeny
tiny

BOO!

SLIDING

A
Shadowy
Someone,
Stepping
Softer
Than
Mouse,
Is
Creeping
Into
The
Firehouse.

Someone's
Chuckling.
Upon
My
Soul!
Someone
Is
Sliding
UP
The
Pole.

I NEVER SAW

I never saw
                a ghost on stilts
a witch wrapped up
                in patchwork quilts
a dragon
in a wagon
or a wizard wearing kilts.

I said
I never *did*.
I didn't say
I never *may*.

THE WITCH'S GARDEN

In the witch's
garden
the gate is open
wide.

"Come inside,"
says the
witch.
"Dears,
come inside.

No flowers
in MY garden,
nothing mint-y
nothing chive-y

Come inside,
come inside.
See my lovely
poison ivy."